To the Grave

AMANDA BRUNS-MILLS "AB"

Fulton Books
Meadville, PA

Published by Fulton Books 2024

ISBN 979-8-89221-024-9 (paperback)
ISBN 979-8-89221-025-6 (digital)

Printed in the United States of America

To my daughters, Nylah and Noella, who give me life and strength every single day and for the love in my heart unconditionally.

Panic Attack

And when the walls come tumbling down and I fall face-first to the
  ground, surreal is the *pain*
Engulfing my soul in sharp flames, and my last breath is drained
I cannot beg you
I know my worth
Yet here I am in so much hurt
I wish you knew what you did to me
I don't know why I think you'd care
You're selfish and harmful
But I still love you
Even from there
But the walls just continue to fall
Crushing my self-worth, tormenting my soul
I have to wonder
Are you even still here at all

The Haunting

Your ghost haunts my soul
Moaning promises
In my ear
I know it's a lie, but I still
Choose to hear
I want to keep you closer
Keep you here
Just a bit longer
Feel your warmth from the
Lit fire
Beneath my skin into my soul

WTF

He loves me
You don't
He will fight for me
You won't
Being in his arms is safe and secure
But my heart and mind only want yours
What the fuck is wrong with me? You are not mine in all the ways
Yet there is something there that won't let me look or walk away
I can ignore you and stay away, but you are still right in my mind all
the days
I told you I go all in and don't do things halfway, but when you were
done, how can you just walk away?
This hurts in a way I thought I'd never hurt again; deep pains of
emptiness cut through my skin into my soul like tears of our sin
I miss you so much it is literally insane
I cannot believe I let you in; it's like you are running through my
veins
I don't believe you aren't affected and you aren't as messed up over
this as I am
You won't let me through those walls because you are trying to be the
tough man
I am here, and you are there, and whatever that means, I can't forget
you, and it's in this deep sorrowful hole I remain
Just here in my self-created pain

Stop

But I've seen it in your eyes
I know you feel it too
I didn't know it'd be like this
There's more to me and you
And I don't want to stop you

Whispering Oaks

I am trying so hard to leave you alone, but there's so much that I
    wanna say
So much that I want to do, and the worst of it all is that I know you
    want it too
But you've asked me to stay away, so that's what I'm gonna do
Now it's all up to you
I hope you hear my whispers as I try to call to you
I hope you yearn for my contact because if you want it, I'll come
    through
You are part of my every desire
All while I feel like I'm burning in fire
Holding out hope we will meet again
I told you I'd even be your friend

Letters of Your Name

Your name's on it
They are starting to fall
Off me onto the ground
Or the air
Doesn't matter
I think I am starting not to care
Your mark, your name, your taste, your fingerprints
Some of the things my body used to bare
I thought I understood where you were coming from and I could see
    past that place
But now I just feel indifferent to how you've allowed all this cold
    space
I am no longer staying there
Your marks are now scars, your taste isn't here, your fingerprints
    faded, and the letters are falling off Your name
I would've done it all to keep you happy, but you did this…you are
    to blame
Now my body is losing the letters of your name

Just Stay

It hurts my soul
It rips my heart
When we are this far apart
I don't believe it's over
This can't be how it ends
Not after as far as I let you in
You get mad at me because you have feelings too
I get you don't want them
It'd be best to stay away
But when you think of me, you always come back to play
And I told you, for me, right now, it's okay
Just stay

You Know This

Don't leave things like this
Please talk to me
You don't hurt someone you want to keep
You do them right and let fate decide if they stay or leave
You know this
You make excuse after excuse, but at the end of it, we are still
    connected
You know this
We are a match
That's not going away
You know this
Accept it
You are *destroying me*
You know this
You are not a scapegoat
You know this
Keep me too
And let me see you
You are my boo

That's All

I didn't ask for much
I really didn't
I couldn't; you wouldn't let me
I tried to live in the moment
Our moments
And just let things be
I didn't write the rules, but I wanted to play your game
To me, it wasn't a game
And I thought you felt the same
Each time it got worse
All I wanted was for you and I to
Immerse
Into a place where we could be
Free of all the other things
That keep us separated
I didn't mean to make you aggravated
Now it's all different, and I just want you to be back
But you won't
And it hurts, and
I'm broke, and you need to know you are being a jerk
That's all

You Called Me an Accident

I am I and you are you
Nothing has changed
Whatever we were to each other, we still are
An accident is not what this is
We happened in the most random of ways
I really don't think we had control over our connection; that is the
    universe
Then we are constantly drawn back to each other despite our
    circumstances
You can deny me and push me away, but yes
I am still right here because I already know
And that won't change

224

The calmness
Your presence
Your embrace
Your tenderness
Your caresses
Your kisses
Your longing
Your timeliness
Your attention
So careful
So meaningful
So many things in that place
In those moments
Forever soul tied to me
You were left wondering what more could be, and I still want more
But for now
I know we are left
With just that memory
Because you said you are done with me

Here I Am

I'm not his anymore
But you are still hers
I am okay with the scraps and pieces of you that I can have
And *that* is the most fucked up thing/place I've been
Yet here I *am*
I am worth more
I know that from within my core
I wish you'd just see
All that's here…Just believe that you can be with me

Permanent

My heart is pounding
My throat feels tight
I can't breathe
I can't think
This can't be right
Everything was fine
It was going all right
Then there was a shift
It happened overnight
What you don't understand
And what I'm scared for you to see
Is that you are permanent
Permanent to me
You lit my mind, body, heart, and soul on fire
You come and go from me, but you remain my one and only desire
It's lasting; it's not going away
I've tried…you've tried
Honestly, some days when you go, I just want to die
You are a scar that will never go away
You last; you continue; you remain unchanged
Even at the end of the worst day
You—I cannot erase
To remember you, I'll take that pain
Permanent, you remain unchanged
An accident I could never say
Even if the pain would be void, I'll keep it
I want those memories to stay
My stomach is sick

I can't breathe
I wish you could see
You are…permanent
Permanent to me

Keep Me

First you were a distraction
Then you were an escape
Next you became a frequent thought
And nightly dream about your face
I never thought I'd be an instead of
Always knew I was an addition to
That's why I can't understand you being done when I said
You can keep me too

Emptiness

The emptiness
The uncertainty
The shakiness
The uneasiness
All rolls on when you stop
The seen and read
But no response
The ignoring
The hurt
The pain
The tears
The sting
It doesn't go away
It gets worse each second of each day
Why does it have to be this way
You want me
I want you
See me
Breathe with me a little bit longer
It just can't be through
Please

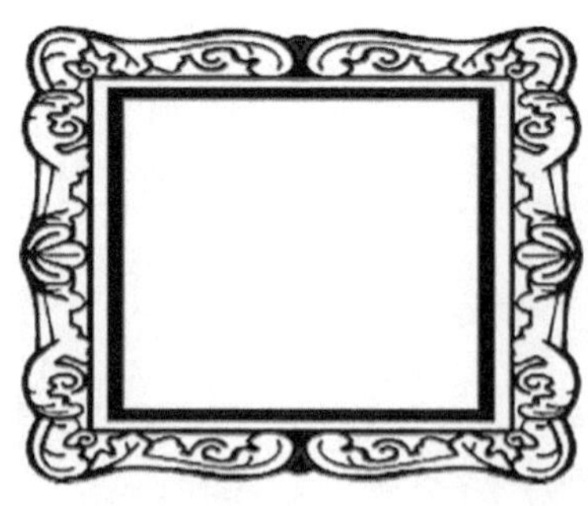

Private Story

I feel so low
It's so heavy
The bricks on my chest keep me down
To my face, a blow
A sucker punch to the stomach
I swear I am going to drown
In this place I keep coming to
Now matter how hard I try
No matter what I do
You find a way to put me here
To destroy me and make me cry
I would give you everything
It's all right here waiting
But you refuse—you deny
The magic of my soul is dying
I don't know how long I can keep trying
So instead I'll just be here
Right where you left me
Waiting for you to accept
This destiny
Or for me to accept this tragedy
Whatever it is, I really don't care
I don't need a label
We are tied; we are attached
I know it's not the idea of stable
But it is real
Not a fiction
Not a fairy tale
And for all those reasons, I am still right here

Lit

When darkness falls and the angels are silent
I look for you in the depths of the sullen night
The world is on fire and tears are falling
I don't understand how our souls are united
I've fallen so hard, but now I'm crawling
Into this cold place where you have left
Me down in the deep—down in the depths
I keep reaching; I'm not giving up
But when I touch you, I can never seem to keep you long enough
Before you leave me once again
I just don't understand
I cry out for help; I want to be enough
But here I am burning, and the angels are silent
Now you feel so violent
Come back—bite my lip and my clit
It's you who keeps me lit

Checkmate

You are my fire, my flame
Yet also my pain
I know the part I play in my own suffering
But I am still here
I remain
This is permanent
This is stained
And honestly, I don't want it to change because then I'd lose you, and
    that is not okay
So I guess I'm your chess pawn, and you can keep using me as part
    of your game
But remember, we all fall down, and you know the way we *both* feel
    is to blame

Gone

Just like that, you left
One last breath
Forever gone
I can only imagine your beauty there
Radiance
Your footprints are still here
Thinking of our last moment
Which I did not know that's what is was, but it was good
You are good and pure
You know it's bad when the music is silent
It hurts, but you don't
And that is my only takeaway
No more pain

Blocked

You would not be able to look me in my eyes
You yelled, cussed, and, worst of all
Didn't even say goodbye
Blocked
I feel absolute pain in my core
And you had just left my body devoured and sore
Then, like that, my entire soul is lying on the floor
I know you are mad, mad that you think of me
I know you are torn because there are parts of you that want us to be
I understand the place you are
And I know the place I am
Wish I knew how to close that gap
How to get you to see that you can act
We can find a way; it will be slow
Maybe it's better that way, though
But there is literally nothing I can do
Blocked

Stained

Look at me
Tell me what you see
Tell my life
What do you think
Privilege?
You are wrong
Trauma runs through my veins
Deep is pain
It's left a stain
I scrub and scrub
And at times it fades
But the truth is
It will never go away
I let you in to see it
Only because I thought you'd stay
But even you left
They all go away
And I am still here
Stained

Not Yet

You ain't done with me
I see it in your eyes
And neither am I
We just don't know how to make it work with our lives
If only we could both agree to jump in
Just dive
Crazy thing to want to be with you like this
It's insane the things I am willing to miss
To take a chance to be with you
The fire burns through and through
You have changed every part of me
As I have you
You are so resistant to accept things as they are
So I'll be here waiting again with your scars

Rock Bottom

I keep searching
Reaching down with my feet as far as I can go
As long as I can hold my breath, I try to reach as far as I can with
    my toes
I can't find the bottom
I can't feel it or sense it
But I know it's there
Somewhere
I want to stop falling
Maybe then I'll be free
When I reach rock bottom
Where it's too dark to see
The panic and fear
That, for so long, I hold
I wonder if the anxiety will be gone
Even if it's cold
Then maybe I can focus
On the climb up ahead
Maybe I'll be content
No longer feel dead
The guilt I've held
Deep inside for so long
Will it recede
I accepted my wrong
I want to be done with the tears and shame
Not reachable anymore
No more stuck in between
Or dying on the floor
I think when I'm there
I can push back with my feet

Then maybe I can have movement
My two pillars can finally meet
I don't know if this is the hell at the bottom or the top
But I've been here too long
It's been nonstop
Never knew I'd seek rock bottom

Suffocating

I can't breathe
The pressure is suffocating
I feel it rise from my stomach to my chest
Tight around my throat
I use my self-talk at my best
But it's not enough
There's not much of me left
I can't hold on forever
I want to die
All I want is you
Again by my side
Just please look me in my eyes
It's different when you do
You know it's true
I am not the same without you

I'm Sorry

If you could see my eyes
I'd show you my soul
Let you look deep within
Finally, you would know
I would never mean to hurt
Disappoint or impose
There's so much I hold back
That I have not felt safe to disclose
Now I understand I caused
Pain your way
I will show you everything
Please let me stay
I am so sorry I did that
I'll make it up in every way
Knowing you will let me try
Don't let this be goodbye
You can trust that I am true
Let me make it up to you

Fail

The thing is
I never wanted to disappoint you
Never meant to let you down
I only wanted to bring you up
So you'd want our moments to keep coming around
I caused you pain
I can't change that fact
To me, this is not a game
But I want you to know I would never stab you in the back
I'm so sorry I let you down
Yet when I can feel your hurt
I know something is there
We both do care
So don't step away
Come closer instead
I will obey
Wonder what it'd be like to know all the thoughts in your head
So we didn't have to choose what to keep and what to say
Because you know I'm in it
I'm here to stay

You Are Just Gone

Damn, I can't even explain the way it feels
Knowing I still can't come to a way to heal
You're gone, and I still don't know why
You were taken too soon, no goodbye
It's been a lot of, with you, years
Now getting swallowed by hurt and fallen tears
No way to heal when justice hasn't had its way
He's still out there living his days
He's free, and you're ashes in a box
There at heaven's door when it knocks
Stuck in this hurt-filled place
Stuck with that image of your broken face
It was so clear that something wasn't right
You were so strong, definitely put up a fight
He may have broken your body
Left you bloody, lifeless, and cracked on the floor
But he could not take your soul
Even though things were tore
Apart and never again be whole
But you are no longer a pawn
Now you are just gone
Grief is this empty space
No words for the pain of a lost embrace
You are just gone

She, Me, We

I guess I did not know how hard this would be
Sitting here alone, looking at the shes and mes
You told me you were upfront
But then there were moments, our moments, that made me believe
What we felt could be more than what we could see
And I want us to be
I would jump with you right now, jump with both feet
I would swim so far away and go with you so deep
But I am starting to see that's not what you're going to be
Then I am stuck looking at this "we"
It intoxicates me, makes it hard to breathe
It has changed my entire world and literally broken me
But I want you, you are always on my mind
I cannot remember a time that I felt this blind
And weak, anxious, a total mess, and incomplete
Until the times that our lips finally meet
Then that all goes away, and it feels like magic
At times I wonder are you even real but then it
Turns so tragic
I want to change the pattern
I want this match to always burn
No more she and me
Instead, it's *we*, you and me

Same

I remain the same
I am not a fiction
I am not a fairy tale
I said I would go by your terms
I am real
I don't ask for anything from you
But a little time and attention
And I'm still right here
I am real, and I don't leave
You hurt
You sting
You caused me misery
But I stay
I remain
I am a stain
Still here, still the same
There is nothing here on me to place blame
I love you
I am not ashamed

Ghost

There were times that I need you the most
You left me there alone, alone with your ghost
For so long, you put distance between us, and it literally felt like
eternity
But yet when you come back, lock me to you and throw away the key
We were strangers, and then in one kiss, it all became true that you
were for me and I for you
Yet you get scared and cut me off and knock me down over and over
again
But here I still am—still here—it's just so destructive
Like a moth to a flame that burns its wings
I keep coming back to you, and it brings
Slavery, I'm sick; I'm an addict for you to do as you wish
You destroy me every time as I fall helpless in your arms, your body,
and your eyes
All to be ravished for minutes and then abandoned in lies
Why? I ask myself each and every time
But I'm still right here even though you ain't mine
I like you, I love you, I want you; I need you in my life
Even if it's me, your ghost—and your wife

A Place

I'm at this place; you are not here
I feel you're sad, but I never see your tears
You told me before it's not me who's caused you this pain
But you shut me out, so here I am again wondering
I'm sorry for any wrong I've ever done to you, never my intent
Only want to keep you close, not on the defense
Let your guard down with me; I'm not going anywhere
This is the only way you'll see I am here
It can't get much worse
I know I am on the side of the blessing
Absolutely not the curse
Come see the things I bring
Make a place and stay with me

Match

Little pieces of you are everywhere
Floating in the air
I breathe you in, and I don't want to breathe you out
I want to keep you there
I'm not ready to let you go, so if you push, I'm not going to give in
You are something that I never want to end
I don't have to put a label on it
It is what it is
But I crave every second of you
And I wish you'd accept me and just finally admit
We are a match
That is a fact
There really is no turning back

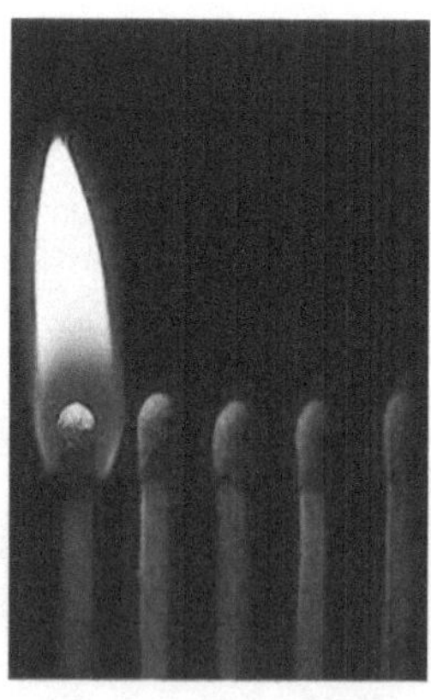

Changing Me

I miss you in a way
A way that's changing me
It hits me hard
Weak in my knees
You create distance, say it's to protect me
I don't feel that way
It's not safety
The highs and the lows
Grip my throat
Suffocating
My tears are hot on my face
Excruciating
I think you see me and even
Feel my affliction
So if you care
Why the constant and then
A sudden restriction
Brutally broken yet you are missed miserably
But it's cutting constantly
I miss you in a way that's changing me
A way that is starting to erase everything

A

Tear-stained face
Lost smiles
My heart fell so fast
I don't think I'll survive
Another cutoff and for what
Is not even clear
I am so hurt, but I just keep
Standing here
I don't want to move away
I just want you to stay
I scare you because I won't leave
You push and push, but I believe
I would wear the scarlet letter for you
I'd burn until each flame was through
I didn't even see you coming, but you engulfed my soul
And you are unlike anything I will ever again know
So you tell me how we let this go

More

I feel invisible
See through, clear
I think I am transparent
But in an honest way
Not a liar, as you say
Broken down
Your words shatter
My heart and soul
You know how to
Hit my core
Why would you not want
More

There

The lower we fall, the closer we are to the void and the ghosts that
    wish to drag us in and eat us there
And you say you don't care
I'm right here naked and bare
If it's hell at this point, I do not even care
I will stay here
I have no fear
Bring me to my final despair

Naked

I saw the parts of you
The parts you hate
But I don't
You see, that's the thing
I accept all of you, and
I'm actually honored to see the broken, angry, hurt pieces of you
Not to fix them like you think but
To be in it with you
When will you see I'm not fighting against you
I am standing beside you, bracing tightly for
Whatever is to come
It's not the naked with your clothes that got me
It's your naked soul and
Admiring how it glows
I'm not here to run away
I'm here to stay

Blood

I wear my heart on my sleeve
You get what you see
My doors are usually open
I don't like them closed
Instead of judging you, I try to imagine the reasons
Of the choices you choose
So here we both are with everything to lose
You quit and walk away but
Come back because you know I stayed
One day, I won't; I'll reach my limitless ends
And then I hope you remember how far I was
Willing to bend—until I broke, and you still walked away
Leaving me bleeding from the sins

Combat

All I wanted was to be happy with you
You keep hurting me and ripping me down
You really want me to go way
Look
There is nothing I want more than you
We are not done
You know it
I'm here like usual
Waiting for you
Even though you keep resisting me
I have not found my reason to walk away
Instead, I feel drawn to you
Just wait and you'll see
I am worthy
I am enough
Just let me stay and earn your trust
I won't hurt you; I know that
You are too rare
Let me try with you
Never take you to combat
You are worth so much more than that

Whore

You make me feel like a whore
It hits deep, and a piece of my soul, you tore
Devalued, demoralized, shamed
Yet I did nothing that warrants any blame
I deserve to be treated better
Believe me, I know
It's not the way I wanted things to go
Yet still here I am with you in my head
And thoughts of keeping you in my bed

RIP

My soul feels torn bit by bit
Each time you ignore my attempt
I see you, but you don't see me
I reach for you, only to grasp open space between
But I know you are and the feelings are there
Is that the struggle of dealing with the affair
Pieces of me are being ripped apart from my soul, my worth, and
    my heart
I can't explain the connection that we share, but I know
You are not feeling less
I'm so confused why you shut me out; do you want us to cease to
    exist
Why can't you tell me if you want things to shift
Silence is the worst hurt
Silence is my pain
Silence is the RIP

Always on My Mind

Sometimes, I wonder
Wonder what your thoughts are
If I'm in them
If you remember me at all
If you miss me
If you want me
My life has changed in so many ways, but you are still there
I think of you
I remember you
I miss you
I want you
You have become part of me so quickly
And there is so much I still don't even know or understand
But the butterflies never go away
You are always in my head, and I like it
I want more
Always on my mind

Walls

You do this every time, and it keeps getting worse
Your walls get taller, and I can't take it anymore
We bared our souls and joined together in that place
Now it's like you just stopped without a trace
I just want to look at you in those eyes with your soft skin by mine
Because then I know your resistance will fall and
Then I can see the real you that you are

Void

Now that you are gone, there is this emptiness
I felt it instantly like when you must have decided
A blank spot in my soul—in my every day
Simple things, really, the messages, the check-ins, the pics—they just
    stopped
I'm not sure what happened to make things change
I wasn't done, and I was still having fun
I miss your soft skin, your deep, dark eyes, your kisses
That made me shake, and even your attempts to push me way and
    my way to pull you closer
But now you are gone, and I'm left with this—this silence, this
    nothingness
It is painful
This *void*

Just Wait

I see you, but you don't see me
You aren't even looking
How do you do that
Tell me how you feel
Please talk to me; hate your silence
Your no responses
Your opened and read messages
I'm trying to give you space, but
It's driving me insane
I need closure to move on
Can you at least give me that
One last face-to-face
Soul to soul
Body to body
I know you are looking
And I'm standing right here
There is a place for us—I know it
There has to be
Magic isn't made to be hidden
It isn't felt often
I need it back
And will find a way again
Just wait and see

You

I drove through a red light on purpose today.
I don't think I'm going to be okay.
Glass Coke bottles,
Smart water,
Plastic key cards
Feel like manslaughter.
You made me feel seen, loved, and like a model
So much I looked past too many disregards,
Then breathed a life into me I never knew existed
Yet ripped it all away and only resisted
My attempts, efforts, reaches, and outpouring of the imprinted love
    and adoration.
Now I'm sitting alone in damnation.
Climbed those walls over the top and then jumped down inside.
Made a home there where I vowed to apply
Everything I am; I'll be right there with you.
I can only hope it eventually soaks through.
I am nothing anymore.
I am just *you*.

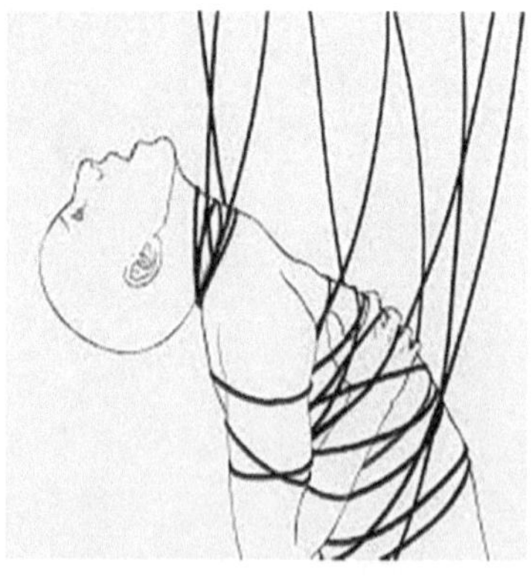

The Fall

The lower we fall, the closer we are to fulfilling the void
And the ghosts that wish to drag us in and eat us there
And you say you don't care
I'm right here naked and bare
If it's hell at this point, I do not even care
I will stay here
Keep tongue-kissing with death
Holding hands into hell
Everyone can tell
All because of the fall
It's tragic and magical
Landing on the greatest love of all
That was and is and is and is
I am forever his
But he was never mine
Brutalist story of all time
Where is the line

The Grave

I am enamored
By the way the air makes electricity between us
Moments before our mouths collide.

I have never in my whole life
Been kissed like this.
It is worth losing everything to be with you,
Be loved by you,
Get lost in you.
Our bones are in this grave you dug for us,
Enamored on our tombstone,
To the grave.

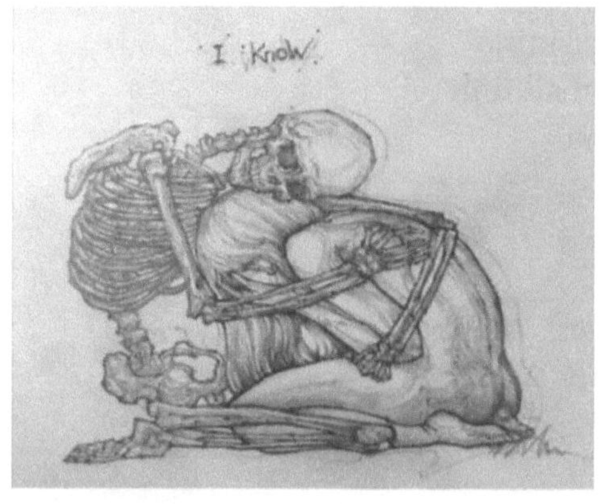

The End

When it is over
I hope you know
I wept from the depths of my soul
My heart was ripped in so many ways
I don't let people in unless they are to stay
You broke down my walls and begged to come in
Then, once inside, destroyed me from within
It really wasn't necessary, but you tore me to shreds
Now all I want to be is dead
Nothing makes me happy
I can't get that smile
I never knew I was even lonely until
You arrived
But then you left, and I am a mess
Trying to find anything of me that is still intact
I want to go on
To end this life
So there it is
While you stay with your wife
I want you to know I love you in every which way
I meant when I said I'd take it to the grave
All I ever wanted was for you to not go all the way away
Just to stay
Now I say goodbye
I don't think I could even look at you in your gorgeous eyes
I guess this is it this time because now I am gone
Risked and lost it all—so withdrawn
The pain is too immense that I can no longer pretend
So that is it
This is the end

Enamored

I'm enamored to your love
Endeared to your arms
You are the other half of my glove
Spellbound by your charm

Enthralled by you
Breathless to my tomb
I will never run away
You will never have to assume

My love for you runs deep
My soul is yours to keep
Forever devoted to you
Enamored to you

Static apnea

Its a good thing I can hold my breath for so long
Under the water and my body and mind are so strong
My heart though
Its weakened I can't find a pulse
My soul ripped to shreds
I've lost all impulse
Of life and smiles and love
I can't breathe
Stretching out for my other glove
Dead roses
Empty bed
I needed to be chosen
And now I am
Dead

Revelation

Took me by surprise
Hazel eyes and a huge grin
Rooftop fireworks
Safe arms
Warm skin
Two cancelled plane tickets
Bright lights and ringing bells
Adventures full of life
Swirling numbers and tornados
Words and feelings we didn't tell
Trying to give you time
Hoping you'd see
Everyone has ghosts
But with you is where I want to be
The haunting will stop
You are a revelation for me
Just Don't leave

About the Author

Amanda Bruns-Mills "AB" is a deeply empathetic person who writes about past and current personal experiences, as well as the pain of others. Her hope is that the deep, dark vulnerability encourages others that they are not alone by articulating emotions that are often hard to connect to. Writing helps cope with these feelings and encourages others into survival by sharing feelings and stories. She is a voice of a survivor, an advocate and mental health therapist.

She lives in East Tennessee with her two beautiful daughters, Nylah and Noella.

There is beauty in the depths of sorrow.